DIRECTLY FROM THE
Heart

TARUN K DABRAL

First Published in January 2022

ISBN: 978-93-5472-947-8

BLUEROSE PUBLISHERS

www.bluerosepublishers.com

info@bluerosepublishers.com

+91 8882 898 898

Cover Design:

Muskan Sachdeva

Typographic Design:

Ilma Mirza

Distributed by: BlueRose, Amazon, Flipkart

Dedicated To

My Lord Shiva (Shri Vansheshwar Mahadev Ji).
My loving parents and to all my family members.
My wife Sheepika Sharma Dabral.
My baby boy Arindam Dabral.

Our Late Bollywood Actor Mr. Sushant Singh Rajput.
Those innocent people who left this world during the severe impact of Covid-19 pandemic.

Acknowledgement

I'm presenting my wholeheartedly felicitation to my Lord Shiva (Shri Vansheshwar Mahadev Ji) who always enlightened me with deep knowledge, inner motivation with high level of mental and physical strength to write this book.

Along with this my special thanks to my loving parents, to all my family members, colleagues and friends for giving me such a big helping hands and motivation to accomplish this project which was totally impossible without their cooperation.

A heartily thanks to my loving wife whose valuable ideas, motivational thoughts and amendments to my work inspired me to complete this work in a more beautiful way. She is not only acted as my wife but also acted as a true friend through the complete journey of writing this book.

Last but not the least a lovely thanks to all my readers who showed interest in my book. This book of mine will surely connect you to the reality of today's world and will inject a full flash positivity in you. I'm obliged.

Thanks To:

All my readers for their extreme love and support.

My Lord Shiva whose blessings and enlightenment is always with me.

My parents and to all my family members.

My wife Sheepika, who was always with me during the journey of writing this book.

Blue Rose Publishers who showed interest in my writing to take my ideas, thoughts and personal experiences to the whole world.

Preface

Hello! My dear and near ones. I'm here putting my ideas, thoughts and personal experiences before you in the form of this book. Actually I have been working on this poetry work since 2010. Many ups and downs in my life after the completion of my schooling jostled me to write this work. But due to some personal reasons I couldn't get my work published on time.

Now, with full enthusiasm and positive energy I'm here before you. This work of mine is totally based on my thoughts and personal experiences that I've perceived from my day to day life.

And most of my creations in this book are based on the real life experiences that forced me to present this work before you. In this modern time and modern lifestyle of hustle and bustle where everyone wants peace of mind but unable to get it so. So, this is my little effort to show you a bit reality of today's life and the right path that you have to choose in this modern time to sustain a stable life. If you go through this book thoroughly, I hope you'll surely get some solutions to get rid of the side-effects of this modern time. Seeking for intense love and support from all my lovely readers to this book.

Wishing all of you a healthy and bright future ahead.

Author's Introduction

I, Tarun Kumar Dabral hold a Master's degree in English Literature along with Bachelor's degree in Education. Currently, I'm in a teaching profession and have been serving in S.G.R.R Education Mission for more than four years.

I've also started my two YouTube channels out of which one is named after my baby boy Arindam i.e. Arindam English Speaking Classes. This channel I have started to fulfill the needs of today's children in order to get a better command over English learning and speaking.

One more YouTube channel I've started named English Literature Hub. This one is for those aspirants who are preparing for English Literature and Grammar based competitive exams for the post of LT, TGT and PGT in KVS, NVS, UPSESSB, UPPSC, UKPSC, and UKSSSC Exams.

I'm here to write this book not to just get it published for the sake of money and popularity but to empower my readers to visualize the reality of this modern time.

By this little effort of mine, my readers will surely get something that would really excite their minds and propel their souls in order to make them aware of all positive and negative sides of human beings and modern lifestyle.

And this collection of poems will definitely touch the hearts of all youngsters and evergreen hearts of all old ages also and will boost their excitements to the next level.

Hoping for the best response from your side to this book. Love you all.

Table of Contents

Covid-19: A Severe Pandemic

Never ever thought of this *pandemic*

All were ordered before, all were *systematic*

But, now, all we're and around us

Totally *static*, and our lives now totally *hectic*.

Who thought there would be *new normal*

That would make our lives totally abnormal

Never thought there would be a long queue outside hospital

Abruptly changed all lives from casual to formal.

Globally its hit was *sudden*

Never gave us chance to stand by, proved itself on humanity a *burden*;

Hustle -bustle it created around us

No one was pre-prepared for this action.

Many lost their loved ones

Many lost their own lives

Humans were home-captivated, animal roams and bird flies

Noise of escaped souls all around and shrill cries.

'Statutory Warning' were placed everywhere

Nobody could roam here and there.

One thing, it made us understood

We're nothing but a combo of *Bone* and *Flesh*

God is supreme after all; we're just like small crushable eggs.

Eternal Love, Eternal Relationship

Never matter how obstacles play *puzzle* with us

Our tuning will go on till *doomsday*, like Bee's morning buzz.

For us little Stars are *'Twinkling'*

Moon throwing its 'White Beauty'

Sun is *'Shining'* for us

Universe bowing before us like *'Saturn's ring'*.

The whole universe is *Materialistic*

But our 'Love and Relationship' is worth *Spiritualistic.*

World is running before all silly matters

Don't they know soon it shatters?

But I'm running after you, my Life!

Front liner you're I'm totally behind you, my wife!

Our relationship can't be bound within the boundaries of Hug Day, Rose Day or Valentine's Day

"You make my day", I firmly say, I wholeheartedly say; I make your day, this will go on Every day! Every day! Every day!

Final Departure

Same time but totally opposite as well as heart throbbing!

One side, a lass getting lifelong knot with her beloved

Other side, she continuously mourning for her lifelong detachment from her heavenly settled spouse.

One side, bride waiting for his groom's arrival dressed in marriage wardrobe

Other side, her hubby was coming in white cerecloths.

Quite heart- churning it's my lord!

Now finally he arrived in evening and cheered her and all

Other side, he made her weep and spread there an intense pall.

Again saying I'm dear God!

Same time but totally opposite as well as heart throbbing!

All cheered, danced and enjoyed with him and her, one side

Just opposite totally, all sat around his icy-cooled body that lay died.

Now, next day morning all customs and rituals completed when

She along with her hubby returning to her in-laws then

Other side, leaving his life journey in middle

Leaving to graveyard encircled all his family members in perplexing riddle.

On one side, she's now at groom's door

All were mesmerized with her beauty and welcomed her with inner core

Other side, he enters the land of grave

All souls welcomed him to God's enslave.

Now, she entered a whole new world

For her, all flags of love unfurled

Now, her life is a mixture of up and down

But, overall it's a fun like clown in a big town.

Other side, his body got buried and ashes got mixed in the *Earth*

Then it was poured into holy water and at last it left one *Dearth*

Now there is complete Silence

Now he is free from all *Chaos*, his *Family* and *Earthly Violence*.

Fire Your Ambition

Give your both wings a *Fire*

Give a *spark* to your *Desire*;

Never be lethargic, never be down

Be patient; try again and again to embrace your Platinum crown.

Listen only to your heart

Let's others' negativity a big dart;

It's your life; others' interruption is not at all accepted

Don't let others your all senses to be captivated.

Others only backbite

Will never throw on you a single positive advice;

It's your life, only you have to give it a hard push

Don't let it dwell in marshy bush.

Never let yourself down before odd people and miserable circumstances

Set an example for others, be a sprouted branches;

Don't underestimate that you can't earn the fame

Keep a fair distance from all disgusting people; surely you'll earn career and name.

Your thinking and inner motivation will definitely give you a fearless fly

Say to your all problems a big – Bye! Bye!

Be *Industrious* and *Nurture* your future, surely you'll break all limits of sky.

Surely you'll break all limits of sky!

Surely you'll break all limits of sky!

Hard Work—A Way to Success

So many sacrifices, so much pain
Without pain, not a single gain.

Getting early in the morning
Take our sleeping to churning;
Squeezing and result come then.

A lot of here and there
A lot of ups and downs
Without extra efforts unable to get crowns;
Getting success isn't an easy job.

Sometimes heads get on swinging
But can't tell anyone anything;
Never underestimate yourself.

To get success, not know, when we commit mistakes

But sometimes whole life it shakes.

Success demands *Activeness*, *Rigidness* and *Continuity*

To touch success, every time we need *Puberty*.

Laying yourself down before someone, who is flapdoodle and mean

Totally helpless condition we seen.

Sometimes bodies work but minds fail

At one time, into ocean of problems, we're drowning

Next time, on ocean of opportunities, we sail;

Getting success isn't an easy job.

At one side, problems squeeze out all our life juice

Other side *Patience*, *Positivity*, *Stability* in us they infuse

To touch the apex, hard work motivates us from inside

Success will sound itself all around but hard work from others you must confide.

Hoppers' Call

Was busy in my work
Heard hoppers' soothing call
Broken silence reached my ears;
Something they want to say.

Think they enjoying summer evening
Or calling their beloveds
Or have something to convey;
Not really understood.

Hope they would have a mediator
Or convey their longings through interpreter
Or wish we both had same vocal cord;
Keep me among them for always, my lord!

Want to hop here and there
Free from all care;
Want lonely happiness,
Want to live life at the fullest.

They celebrating their emancipated lives

Making me feel jealous;

Can I be like them?

Or be human for all births?

May be one day

Same dialect I will say

Same life I will enjoy;

Among greens I would be green.

Is It Life?

Steadily everyone wandering to and fro

But for which purpose it is never know

Every person in this world

Now, nefarious and inexorable to fulfill his selfishness.

At a moment, our life is full of joy

A bit later, affliction catches us in its web.

Everyone is prey of others

Through enmity and constant rivalry;

Caused by man against mankind.

Fakeness and *Darkness* dissolved in everyone's heart

Even in soul too

Still blaming others

Pure I'm and unkempt are you.

Behind the curtain, we all refraining path of others

But in front we say – Hello! I'm your pursuer.

Not only our mind but even soul gone sluttish for forever

Still in front we say – I'm your well-wisher.

When every second we feel anguish, helpless and pray before almighty God

God politely answers – My son! It's your own fault.

Nobody is completely pious but somehow profane

Not liberal for a second but all time insane.

Everybody cheating, doing fraud

Even not getting afraid from heavenly God.

Why all we behaving like sages?

When corruption and dishonesty grazed all our ages.

Human is wild now and wild is now human

Inside consist of puzzles, incarnated himself as demon.

Modernization made us puck

All childhood, teenage and all ages it suck.

Now war among human-beings is by the human, for the human and limited to the human

Bleeding, murder and destruction is now a big fun.

Seems that everyone's mind is now at occiput

Continuously occluding others' ways, good things to conduct.

All are willing to malefic others every time

Seems we've caught in the essence of wild wine.

As far you go, will never find any honesty and sincerity

Quite unable to find a single sign of humanity.

Every time we're handshaking with incertitude and distrust

The day is near when the pot of inhumanity will surely burst.

Is It Life?

Is It Life?

Is It Life?

Modernity Superseded Morality

No more respect to our moms

No more respect to our dads

No more respect to our elders

No more respect to anyone.

Busy in our own life

By using fingers all five

Neglecting depth of relationship

Just show-off and nothing else;

No feelings for our loved ones.

Today, all we using modern devices

Hey! After all we're 'Modern', don't we?

And chopping our relationships like onion slices.

We are all breathing

But, do we think we're alive?

No, not at all! Our relationships we're mincing.

Mean job with big name

Big show-off to earn fake fame

With others' feeling and lives, aren't we continuously playing a drastic game?

For humanity, isn't it a matter of big shame?

Fake smiles on faces, intense jealousy from inside

Colorful wardrobes on the body, by-heart really *black* we're guys!

Forgetting everyone for the sake of money

Intentionally and continuously walking in darkness at the time of sunny.

Money, money and money all around

No compassion, no faith in relations we found.

How hectic our parents made their lives for our upbringing, do we really know?

Unaware of all these, we're hard and static like snow

Do we have care for our parents?

Obviously- 'No'.

Then why we're teasing them?

We can do live, if we're senseless

But without blessings of our parents and elders

Won't our life be an extreme mess?

'Think over it'.

Parents are not 'Use me' like dustbin

But depth of an ocean of love that's totally unseen;

They aren't like colors those are visible

But like a salt; without them our life is quite infeasible.

Love, Care and Stability all they need at the old age

Just like they looked after us, we must follow the same.

My Mother, My Proud

My love, my *affection*
My mother, my *perfection*.

Thought of her deeply always
When surrounded by *Hardness* of life;
In her absence
My life was really a big *Strife*.

Thank you *Mother* for your presence
Incarnated in guise of god;
With you
My earthly life is now god's abode.

On each and every problem of mine
She threw a Jupiter-sized sunshine;
Made her life *Severe* and *Drastic*
Mine really a big *Divine*.

In summer, my *cotton clothes* she's
In winter, my *woolen clothes*;
In rainy season, my *rain coat*
In flood time, she's my *cruise boat*.

On ground she *held* me tight

My reality when I forgot and flew like a kite;

Saved me from each and every hound

To me when they came to bite.

When *Depressed* rays all around me and created illusions

Surrounded by all obstructions;

All unkempt, all negative she took on her

Made my life all cozy and an extreme fur.

Saved me from every pall

Can't use a single word to describe all;

Removed all obfuscation of my life

Whenever felt low, held me and hugged me tight.

Not with complete maturity but some childishness

Understood with her life's all negativeness;

Blunt-edged totally was my life

Finally, she molded me into a bit sharper knife.

Not Same to Same

Faces not same

Not same the physique

Not same thinking

Not same outlook.

Why it's like this?

Nothing but different all we are

Different people follow different way to live life and behaving with others.

If I'm doing the same then what problem occurs?

From behind the curtain, *Snake-bite* if you give

Then be hard from inside;

I'm not a eunuch;

The same thing you will receive.

You and I

All we are *dwarf-sized* before God;

But our outlook is all different

How could be the same our behavior?

My behavior depends on your attitude

Good before me you are, same I'm with you;

And never expect much from others

Limited expectations infinite ecstasy.

Never sneak peek for others

Everyone has his own feathers; want to fly

Then you must; but interference in others' lives totally intolerable

If can't think *plus* for others, not allowed to think *minus* also.

God blessed me this human incarnation

Never want to lose my happiness with your mean suggestion;

No interference, no problem

If tease you will, surely get an answer.

Always say point to point

Never adhere to any backbite;

If you do so

Won't leave you at any cost, alright?

Never try to *uproot* others
Same thing can happen with you;
If you think I'm unkempt
Not even pious are you.

So never try to meddle
Never try to cheat;
If you propel proper coordination
Always we will be on same floating fleet.

O Rain! O Rain! Please Come Again

O Rain!   O Rain! Please come again, Please come again

Feeling drastic, too hot and sarcastic

Humidity going rise

Sweating coming thrice.

Why are you heating us?

Why are you teasing us?

Don't you know we're feeling suffocation?

On our work unable to make concentration.

If you shower, blessed we feel

When raindrops touch us, inside it create zeal.

Hey! Rain Please come again, Please come again

Not only we but green grasses and plants need you

Not only grasses and plants but animals and insects also appreciate you.

But, please don't fall down too much

Flood it creates, destruction it touch;

And even not fall down too less

First it creates drought then quite unsolvable mess.

Can't scramble layer of summer without you

When you drizzle, always we feel *Zeal, Rejuvenation and New.*

Reason, Reality and Solution

All Things Happen In This *World*
As It Has Reason Behind It.

Nearby us, air blows
Unique power of giving life;
Goes inside our nostrils and life flows.

Sun rises to sustain life on earth
Without it we're unable to take birth.

Moon rises up in night
To fight with darkness for us, makes the night much bright.

Every step towards Science-Inspired future (already aware of its side effects)
Don't we know what will be its conclusion?

All we crave for self-importance, and money in society

But don't think earning is the final pursuit; the thing we need to get by hard work

- Dignity and Stability.

In the race of prestige and money earning

Our souls we continuously burning;

Now, we are numb in this way

Competing with others, whether it's night or day.

Side-effects of Modernization-

It turned everyone

Cruel, unconscious and secluded from other;

Made everyone puck and impossible to live together.

Why make others feel I'm your well-wisher?

Actually in real, only I'm jealous and backbiter.

This *'Modernity'* made our lives fully hectic

Ourselves responsible for this we're and bruised our lives;

And made our lives all septic.

Responsible for self-created surroundings of hustle and bustle

Just for the name of getting self-dependency and to be a great entrepreneur

Now producing panacea for all ours mental and bodily depression

A hectic life is carrying forward as a symbol of the rich's fashion.

Solutions to get rid of Intense Modernity –

Throw all skyscrapers in garbage

Burn all hectic schedules in *altar;*

Never run out of time for your loved ones

It wasn't a part of our *Vedic* culture.

Touch the extremity of generosity

Nurture *Positive Egoism* in your lap

And let it grow;

And keep yourself down to earth in real.

Infuse all positivity in your veins

Help the needy when it's needed with selflessness

Analyze your soul time to time what you sacrificed for others

Repeat it further and further.

And at last phase of life

Leave all luxuries and amenities

Devote yourself to enchanting mantras, spirituality
– a way to Moksha or Nirvana

The *final resolution* for which our supreme God
sent us here.

Success Demands Sacrifices

Thinking of success, simultaneously eye to eye

With enjoyment and excursion; with oneself a defy;

If seriousness missing from the vein,

Totally useless lives we liven.

Not saying, enjoyment mustn't be there

But coordination in hard work and excursion demands equal share;

Went through all the realities of life,

Everyone I tested and suffered all strives.

Must feel extreme odd when wasting the time,

Think it's a serious crime;

Must squeeze ourselves till we get fame,

Not to stop anywhere until we limelight our name.

Not to panic if someone tries to suppress you

And also tries to mitigate you;

Everybody demoralizes you if you follow the hard-work,

When succeed, all they along with you; when fail,
give you a hard jerk.

Some say enjoy your life to forget your pain

Come along with us, don't indulge yourself in
immense strain;

I say then, it's not a bad offer

But think I'm not a big loafer.

Before achieving the goal, not stop I will

Not any future plans, future goal to anyone I
reveal;

Success isn't a land to touch so easily, or a one
night fight

To chase, need in your heart an intense might.

It's really a way to heaven! But needs *Bone-breaking Strives and Hidden Sacrifices.*

But needs *Bone-breaking Strives and Hidden Sacrifices.*

But needs *Bone-breaking Strives and Hidden Sacrifices.*

Suppressing World Depressed Me: A Tribute to Sushant Singh Rajput

Always thought and did positive for others

But nobody understood me;

Thought they, if I could surpass them.

For them, not so easy to compete with me.

It's not so easy to disclose your heart

When people around try to play with you;

Don't think everyone is brave enough to fight back.

Hailed from a small village

Still at the top I was at younger age.

Many tried leg-pulling to make me zero

In spite of this I struggled a lot and made myself Hero;

My rivals couldn't digest it

Anonymous for them I was although.

In 2003, among All India Toppers I was

Physics I liked, drowned into Mechanical Engineering;

Soon kicked off my college life

Left it incomplete in the final, had passion for acting.

Debuted my daily soap in 2008

Very fast I was running ahead of my fate;

All went fabulous

Not knew what was hidden in future's womb?

Hit my Bollywood debut soon

Did my best that I could;

But never knew I'd pay for my honesty

A big price for my sincerity.

Counted people supported me

Many in disguise, behind the curtain, tried to suppress me

At my career's peak, how could they like and tolerate me?

And tried hard to kick me out.

Didn't matter from where I was
Following the right, doing work hard;
Thought nobody would suppress me;
But I was wrong!
Suppressing World Depressed Me.

Whom I'd convey my inner feelings
When felt alone from inside;
Not to perplex my loved ones
Suppressed my emotions.
But Suppressing World Depressed Me.

At last, when not sought any solution
Only felt severe depression;
Just to soothe my body and mind
Decided to leave my all loved ones behind.

Surrendered before myself, surrendered before my problems
Thought myself a sack, inside all worries I kept;
Felt disentangled, committed suicide.
Now, I'm much relaxed.

Now, no more worries

No more hurt

No more competitions & complications

No more new rivalries to start.

The so-called respected people

I'd say – "*Big* names but with *Fake* fames"

Can't disclose their plotting and names;

Won't stay happy throughout their lives

No matter how rich they are; will always be in lifelong strives.

To take such step they forced me

From my family they secluded me.

Now, wherever I'm having detached from my soul

Feeling lighter than before;

Fetterless from all bondages

Now, no suppressions anymore.

Temporal World Never Goes With Us

Whenever I think of *Life*
I count many possibilities
Many positivity, many scopes.

And when I sudden think of *Death*
Nothing comes to my mind
A cold and terrific tomorrow clutches my hand.

A question always strikes my mind
If God has to crush lives
Then why he gives us a *positive* birth?

Why he nourishes us through our parents?
Why he gives us protection always?
Only to take lives of us at the end?

Never understood this cycle of *Life and Death*

Never knows the motto of our *Supreme*

For what purpose we take birth

 And leave this earth?

O God! Tell me why you do this?

From the family when you take back one soul

It throttles all

Don't you think only that soul was everything for the family?

I request if you take life of someone

Do some prior arrangements for his dependents

And give them a big heart to overcome this pain.

Why don't you come to this earth

To ensure us and take u class of all?

To convey - *"This soil is temporal."*

Hey! Humans this soil isn't for you permanently

Visitors only you're, enjoy this beautiful world accordingly;

With your family never connect too deeply.

More connectedness will make you cry more and more and more!

This world is totally temporary for you it's sure.

At last, we must keep this in our mind

This Temporal World Never Goes With Us.

This Temporal World Never Goes With Us.

This Temporal World Never Goes With Us.

www.ingramcontent.com/pod-product-compliance
Lightning Source LLC
Chambersburg PA
CBHW052131150726
48002CB00006B/2574